Original title:
The Island Breeze Beckons

Copyright © 2025 Creative Arts Management OÜ
All rights reserved.

Author: Alexander Thornton
ISBN HARDBACK: 978-1-80581-700-0
ISBN PAPERBACK: 978-1-80581-227-2
ISBN EBOOK: 978-1-80581-700-0

Dance of the Ocean's Breath

The waves do shimmy, oh what a sight,
Flip-flop pirates dance through the night.
Seagulls chirp in a squawky tune,
While crabs in tuxedos join the moon.

Bubbles giggle as they float by,
Fish toss glitter, wave goodbye.
Sandy feet tap out a jolly beat,
As the ocean's breath whispers, "Take a seat!"

Starlit Shores and Soft Sands

Stars are winking, giving a nod,
The gentle waves play peek-a-boo, oh what a plod!
Sandcastles wobble, they start to sway,
As kids run wild, losing the day.

A surfboard floats on a jellyfish ride,
While a crab hosts an impromptu slide.
Under the moon, a silly embrace,
As laughter dances in this strange place.

Refuge in the Rustling Leaves

Pinecone hats on furry heads,
Bunnies hop while the whole world treads.
Squirrel acrobatics, a leafy ballet,
While chipmunks cheer and shout, "Hooray!"

Twirling tendrils of ferns unfurl,
Whispers tickle, a leafy swirl.
Nature's giggles beneath the tree,
Come join the fun, be wild and free!

Harmony with the Horizon

The sun yawns wide, paints the sky,
While dolphins leap and seagulls fly.
The horizon waves, a cheeky grin,
Inviting us to join in the spin.

With laughter bubbling like fizzy drinks,
In colorful shirts, we dance and wink.
The sunset jokes with a playful hue,
As we shimmy on through, just me and you.

Murmurs from the Tidal Shore

Waves whisper secrets on the sand,
Crabs choreograph a dance so grand.
Fishermen argue with slippery fish,
Their grand tales like a tasty dish.

Seagulls squawk about their lost fries,
While sunbathers sport their tan lines and sighs.
Each splash of water throws laughter near,
As dogs chase tails without a fear.

Delight in the Alightening Mist

Misty mornings give a giggly scare,
As joggers slip like they're unaware.
Clouds release their puns in drops,
Who knew puddles would be such props?

Foggy whispers love to tease the trees,
Every rustle caters to the breeze.
Sailboats bob on a comedic wave,
As sailors practice how to behave.

Songbird's Voyage to Tranquility

Birds in hats sing silly tunes,
While crickets talk under bright balloons.
Each flutter holds a note of cheer,
As ducks quack jokes we love to hear.

A parrot's laugh cracks the morning light,
While squirrels juggle in sheer delight.
With wings of green and yellow flair,
They dare to dance without a care.

Fluttering Spirits Amidst the Waves

Kites zoom high with a perfect twirl,
While kids run on the shore in a whirl.
Splashing friends in a frothy fight,
Every soaked grin is sheer delight.

Sandcastles crumble, a royal jest,
As tide pulls treasures from their nest.
Laughter dances on the salty air,
As playful hearts forget their care.

Glide of the Gulls in the Nameless Breeze

Gulls hover and twirl, what a sight,
Swooping for snacks, in broad daylight.
They squawk and they dive, oh what a scene,
Chasing each other, too fast, too keen.

An errant chip flies high in the air,
One gull makes a grab with style and flair.
But oh! What a twist, it lands with a plop,
Much to the laughter of the seaweed crop.

A dance on the waves, they twist and they whirl,
Each one a comedian, each one a pearl.
With wings like a sail, they cartwheel 'round,
Dropping some antics, so silly, so sound.

Under the sun, they hold a grand show,
It's a feathered fiasco, a wacky tableau.
So grab your snacks, join in, don't be shy,
With gulls in the air, it's laughter on high!

Awakening to Coastal Dances

Seagulls squawk as they take flight,
Crabs dance cha-cha in morning light.
Sandcastles rise, then quickly fall,
Who knew tides could have such a ball?

Beach umbrellas flutter like flags,
Little kids giggle, holding their jags.
Sunscreen applied, a slather and smear,
Now who's the lobster? Oh dear, oh dear!

Tides Turning at Sundown

As the sun dips low, the sky turns pink,
A fisherman's catch just might make you wink.
His stories grow taller with each pint he sips,
While his fish tales swim beyond logical trips.

Sandwiches vanish, and so do the fries,
Seagulls squabble, inflating their size.
Beer cans stacked high like sand towers lost,
Who knew chill time could come with a cost?

Embracing the Nautical Pulse

Boats frolic 'round like kids on a swing,
With sails so full, they start to sing.
There's laughter galore on each watercraft,
Who knew the ocean had such a craft?

Fish are jumping, but not in line,
Trying to catch one? Oh, what a crime!
Net entangled, and so is the head,
Oh well, here's hoping it's just a red thread!

Wanderlust of the Serene Coast

Flip-flops lost, it's like a game,
Chasing them down? Oh, what a shame.
Tiny crabs wave, they're smart little things,
While we trip over sand, oh the joy it brings.

Picnic plans go awry with the breeze,
Seagulls swoop low, as if they tease.
Who knew the beach had a sense of play?
We chase away snacks, begging them to stay!

Serenade of Swaying Palms

Palms dance with a giggle, so spry,
While coconuts drop with a sly guy.
Flip-flops squeak with a happy tune,
As crabs do the cha-cha under the moon.

Fish in the sea with a wink and a grin,
Play tag with the waves, let the fun begin!
Seaweed sways like it's in a show,
Cheering on surfers with a wave and a flow.

Echoes of Oceanic Dreams

The gulls squawk loudly, having a laugh,
Stealing sunscreen from your beach path.
A starfish grins under its soft shell,
While jellyfish giggle, oh can't you tell?

Under the sun where the sea is bright,
Sandy toes wiggle with sheer delight.
A sandcastle crowned, proud but unsure,
Looks like it's ready to start a war!

Songs of the Gentle Current

Waves sing a ballad, sweet and soft,
While surfers wipe out, they tumble aloft.
Seashells gossip, they're quite the chat,
While dolphins peek out, loving the spat.

The tide waits patiently, twinkling and keen,
To join in the dance, it's a joyful scene.
Seagulls compete for the best snack to munch,
While crabs form a band for a beachside lunch.

Call of the Salty Horizon

The horizon calls with a cheeky grin,
As beach balls bounce where the laughter begins.
Surfers sip drinks on their colorful boards,
While the sun throws a party, with rays in hoards.

Shells dreaming of treasures, they chime and they sing,
Throwing beach raves, let the bright seaspring!
A lobster dressed fancy moves to the beat,
As crabs breakdance on their wave-tossed feet.

Meditations with the Moonlit Sea

The waves have secrets, they giggle and tease,
They pull at my toes like a playful breeze.
I ponder deep thoughts, but they slip away,
As crabs dance around, and fish join the play.

My mind is a vessel, afloat on the tide,
With seagulls as comedians, a true seaside guide.
They squawk their wise jokes, but I don't understand,
Yet I laugh with the waves, as they tickle the sand.

Beyond the Boundaries of Breath

With each salty gust that whirls 'round my face,
I think of my worries, they're lost in the space.
The dolphins are laughing, they flip and they glide,
While I, just a human, am trying to hide.

I chase after seagulls, and they chase back at me,
They flap their great wings, oh what a sight to see!
Maybe I should join them, just soar and be free,
But all they do is chuckle, right back at me.

Canvas of Serenity in Color

Painting the sunset with hues full of cheer,
As peanut butter sandwiches float in my beer.
The colors collide, oh what a delight,
With laughter and squawks merging day into night.

My canvas is messy, my brush, just a stick,
I accidentally painted a crab; what a trick!
Yet here on the shoreline, no judgment I feel,
Just joy and this laughter, oh what a great deal!

Poetics of the Infinite Oceanscape

The vastness of blue spreads, a puddle of fun,
With fortunes of fish and a boat full of sun.
I dream of a pirate with a treasure map,
But I find only jellyfish, oh what a trap!

Each wave holds a punchline, they crash and they roll,
While I sit with my snacks, just a humorous stroll.
The horizon's my stage, and the gulls sing my song,
In the humor of ocean, it feels like I belong.

Secrets Carried by the Sea Wind

Seagulls squawk with great delight,
While crabs dance under the moonlight.
A fish whispers secrets in the tide,
While surfers tumble, in giggles they glide.

Sandcastles crumble with a squeal,
As waves come crashing, what a deal!
The tide pulls back but leaves a riddle,
A dolphin jumps, oh what a fiddle!

Mermaids laugh with a splashy cheer,
While beach balls bounce, it's all so clear.
The ocean's jokes can be quite absurd,
Like finding sand in your favorite curd.

So gather 'round and raise a cheer,
For salty tales we all hold dear.
With every breeze that tickles your face,
Life's a party in this warm embrace.

Chasing Shadows in Sunlit Sands

Sandy toes and hats askew,
We frolic where the wild waves brew.
Sunburned noses, laughter galore,
As we chase the shadows that dance on the shore.

Buckets and spades become fishy friends,
Even sprightly shells have funny bends.
A crab takes a stroll in a tiny parade,
While sunbathers toss shade for a cool lemonade.

Kites fly high in the ocean breeze,
While folks still argue, 'Was it you or me?'
The sand's a canvas, covered in giggles,
Where beach balls tumble and uncles twiddle.

With every sunset, new antics arise,
As seagulls steal fries, oh the surprise!
Our laughter echoes, sweet and bright,
Chasing shadows until the night.

Rhythm of the Tropical Whisper

Coconut hats and sunscreen smears,
The rhythm of laughter combines with cheers.
A parrot spills tea with a cheeky grin,
As the sun dips down and the fun begins.

Limbo sticks swaying under palm trees,
While kids race by with giggles and wheeze.
The sand almost tickles, a mischievous tease,
As we dance with the crabs, doing what we please.

Drumming on barrels, a carnival sound,
With all of our friends joyfully around.
A pineapple hat flies, caught in a breeze,
It lands on a stranger with perfect ease.

So let's toast our cups to nights made of fun,
With tropical whispers, we're never done.
As the stars twinkle brightly, we'll sway and we'll sing,
In this party of life, let the laughter take wing.

Nautical Notes of Serenity

A boat sails in, but what a scene,
Fish start a concert, if you know what I mean!
The captain's hat's too big for his head,
While the sea plays tunes as we rest, not dread.

With every wave, a note does play,
As jellyfish jiggle in a funny way.
We share our snacks, oh what a treat,
A seagull swoops, and targets our feat!

Shells like trumpets lie on the sand,
Each one whispers secrets, a quirky band.
The tide starts to laugh, oh what a delight,
As we dance and frolic into the night.

So raise your glasses, let kindness prevail,
With nautical notes, we laugh without fail.
For every trip on this woven spree,
Is a song of joy, carried by the sea.

Flourish of Flora in Gentle Touch

In shades of green, a party begins,
Flowers dance wildly, forget all their sins.
They sip morning dew, tell tales of the sun,
As insects drop beats; oh, this is fun!

Petals wear hats made of clouds up above,
Laughing with breezes, they twirl and they shove.
A sunflower jokes with a stocky old fern,
While daisies drop puns, they take a bold turn!

With colors so bright, they flaunt like a clown,
A peony giggles and falls to the ground.
"Help me up!" it cries, as the violets laugh,
These floral friendships, a cheerful life graph!

So come enjoy this garden parade,
Where petals and laughter are lovingly laid.
With nature's own chorus, the giggles unfold,
In this riot of colors, a story retold!

Soft Serenades of Nature's Caress

A bird in a tree wears a tweed little coat,
Sings opera to bees—oh, what a great note!
With squirrels as dancers, they prance and they hop,
The woodland is wild; it just doesn't stop!

The moon winks at critters as night starts to play,
While crickets compose their hip-hopping ballet.
A raccoon's in shades, groove on full display,
He flips with finesse, making shadows sway!

Old owls drop wisdom; it's slightly absurd,
While frogs play charades; they're quite the word herd!
The breeze rolls its laughter through branches so high,
Even fireflies flicker in response to the sky!

So join in the revel; forget the day's grime,
Nature's a jester, always on time.
In harmony's whirl, with chuckles so light,
This serenade of joy makes the stars shine bright!

Nightfall upon Iridescent Shores

As sun dips away, the ocean starts to gleam,
Crabs put on hats; they're part of the theme.
They sashay on sand, all bright and absurd,
Leading the party with laughter unheard!

Seashells gossip and trade their bold tales,
Of ships long gone and their tattered sails.
A starfish plays poker, just out of the tide,
With a wild dolphin, swaggering with pride!

The moon spills its silver upon waves that clap,
While seagulls do stand-up; oh, what a mishap!
They squawk punchlines that make the waves roar,
As evening crafts magic on this bustling shore!

So dance by the sea where the funny bones jive,
Let tickles of foam be the reason you thrive.
When night wraps its arms, don't underestimate,
For here's where the humor makes twilight first-rate!

Reflections in Tidal Pools

In pools left behind by the whims of the tide,
Life flaunts ridiculous, won't even hide.
Shrimps wear small glasses and look quite astute,
While sea stars declare their best fortunes to boot!

A clam steals the show with its glimmering pearl,
And barnacles joke with their crusty old swirl.
They play a quick game, who's the best dresser,
"Oooh, I'm the winner! Look at this mess-er!"

The octopus giggles, it changes its hue,
As it plays hide and seek, "Can you see me too?"
With colors and laughter that twirl in the light,
Even seaweed joins in, feeling warm and bright!

So take a small peek into nature's own glee,
Where silliness lives, 'neath the waves and the sea.
In every reflection, a chuckle will bloom,
In tidal adventures, let joy be your room!

Whispers of the Warm Wind

A gentle whisper, oh so light,
It teases me with pure delight.
It pulls my hat, then plays a trick,
Leaves sand in places, oh that's slick!

The seagulls laugh as they retreat,
Two crabs are dancing on my feet.
They signal me to join their dance,
But I'm too busy—what a prance!

Oh salty air, you dash and tease,
You make me drop my ice cream, please!
With every gust, a giggle grows,
Where whimsy blooms, and laughter flows.

So here I stand, a happy fool,
While nature plays a funny duel.
The warm wind winks, a cheeky friend,
And all my worries, they just bend.

Salt-Kissed Echoes

Salt-kissed whispers swirl around,
They lace my laughter, funny sound.
As waves recite their silly tale,
I chuckle loud, may I prevail!

The fish parade, they wiggle near,
One tried to kiss me—oh dear, fear!
I'm dodging bubbles, dance within,
I trip, I fall—oh where's my gin?

Shells gossip tales of days gone by,
A hermit crab just waved goodbye.
He's got my flip-flop, cheeky flirt,
Sandy footprints, what a smirk!

Echoes dance upon the shore,
With every wave, I laugh some more.
In this chaos, fun unfolds,
With salt-kissed giggles, life beholds.

Serenade of the Sea

The sea serenades with a song,
While I float by, it feels so wrong.
A dolphin pops with a cheeky splash,
It steals my snack—oh what a clash!

The tides toss jokes upon the foam,
As barnacles prepare to roam.
They huddle close, sharing their puns,
With every wave, they're full of fun!

Flip-flops squeak, the rhythm's neat,
My ice cream's melting—what a feat!
Wind whispers secrets to the shells,
And I just laugh at all it tells.

As seaweed dances to the beat,
I'm feeling silly on my feet.
With salty waves and sunlit glee,
This serenade, it sings to me!

Canvas of the Coral

The coral paints a scene so bright,
As fish swim past with pure delight.
A clownfish winks, a jester bold,
It jabs my side—I'm bought, I'm sold!

Anemones sway with soft allure,
Their tickling touch, I can't endure.
They push and pull, a playful tug,
In their green world, I'm a snug bug!

Seashells gossip, tales unfold,
Of swim meets lost and treasures sold.
They call to me, join the charade,
In this coral dance, I'm not dismayed.

With laughter rising with the tide,
In the ocean's arms, I'll safely glide.
This canvas rich with colors bright,
Will paint my day with sheer delight.

Paradise Lost and Found

In a hammock swinging slow,
I spied a crab stealing my toe.
He waved his claws with such glee,
I laughed and said, "Come share my tea!"

Palm trees leaning, quite the sight,
Swaying left, then leaning right.
The sand grins, it knows our game,
Who knew beach life brought such fame?

Seagulls squawked an off-key song,
I danced along, it felt so wrong.
With sunscreen smeared upon my nose,
I sang to fish as they struck poses!

Lemonade spills in the heat's embrace,
It drips and dances all over the place.
Lost my flip-flop, it took a dive,
But oh, the stories that keep it alive!

Whispers of the Coastal Wind

The wind whispered secrets of old,
I listened closely and felt bold.
It teased my hair, gave me a fright,
Then stole my hat and took off in flight!

Sandy toes and laughter shared,
Made friends with a clam, it never cared.
We plotted to catch a wave or two,
But the sneaky tide just laughed at our crew.

A beach ball bounced, out of control,
The dog chased it, what a stroll!
He crashed and tumbled, rolling 'round,
While I just doubled up, joy unbound.

Seashells giggle at the tide,
As we skip stones, hands open wide.
The wind carries our laughter free,
A symphony that lasts, endlessly!

Embrace of the Ocean Air

Caught in a breeze, my hair's a mess,
Like a tumbleweed, I must confess.
The seagulls cackle, their jokes quite lame,
But I laugh back, it's all just a game.

Pretending to swim, I flop like a seal,
A wave crashes down, oh what a squeal!
My sunglasses fly, away they zoom,
While I ponder the ocean's great room.

Children are building a fortress of sand,
With moats and towers, oh isn't it grand!
But when the tide comes, their dreams wash away,
"See you in Lego land!" they cheerfully say.

With ice cream dripped down my side,
I chase a crab as it tries to hide.
The ocean air, a sweet perfume,
Makes this day feel like a living cartoon.

Dancers of the Seaside Zephyr

With seashells clinking like tiny bells,
I twirled 'round, casting all my spells.
The wind joined in, a partner so spry,
It lifted my spirits, oh my oh my!

A sandcastle fell, I let out a yelp,
As a toddler giggled, probably helped.
We rebuilt it with laughter and cheer,
Making memories that will last all year.

Dancing with crabs on the shore so bright,
One stole my snack, what a thrilling fright!
We laughed as he scuttled, proud as can be,
While I pondered if he shared it with glee.

The sun dipped low, painting skies with flair,
As we waved goodbye to day without care.
For tomorrow will bring new tricks and fun,
In this land where joy's never quite done!

Paths of the Wandering Wind

A gust comes by with a tickling laugh,
It steals my hat, oh what a gaffe!
Dancing leaves in a quirky race,
Nature's prankster in this sunny place.

Socks and sandals? What a sight!
Flapping flags wave with delight.
Chasing clouds that look like sheep,
Here's to the day, no need for sleep!

Laughter echoes with every swirl,
Windy winks make my head twirl.
With every blow, a new surprise,
Oh, how wind can tease and rise!

So let's run wild, let spirits soar,
With the playful breezes we adore.
Join the dance, don't be shy,
Embrace the fun as we fly high!

Caress of the Soft Surf

The waves come rolling with a chatty cheer,
Whispering secrets as they draw near.
Sand between toes, oh what a treat,
But watch out now, don't lose your seat!

Seagulls squawk, they steal your fries,
Plotting schemes under sunny skies.
Sunburned noses and laughter loud,
This beach life makes us all so proud!

A splash here, a splash there, oh what fun!
Water fights under the blazing sun.
Sunscreen slathered, all eyes squint,
At this soft surf, we're free to sprint!

So grab your board and take the plunge,
With every wave, we'll laugh and lunge.
Let's make a splash and dance about,
For here's a life that's always in stout!

Mysteries in the Misty Air

Fog rolls in with a silly face,
Hide and seek, it's in this space.
Shapes appear, then quickly fade,
Like magic tricks in a charade.

"Is that a shadow or a ghost?"
I'd rather have pancakes, I do boast!
Misty mornings, what a sight,
Makes my coffee taste just right!

Whispers echo, but what do they say?
Shivers and giggles, oh what a play!
But when it lifts, what will we see?
A seagull stealing my cup of tea!

So let's embrace the foggy glee,
With every mystery, let's just be free.
In the mist, our laughter's bright,
Here's to fun, from day to night!

Voyage into Horizon's Whisper

Sailing out in a rickety boat,
With snacks packed high, I'm set afloat.
Tidal waves give a hearty cheer,
As I tip over, soaked with beer!

My compass spins like a whirling top,
Fish are laughing, I'll never stop.
Lost in thoughts of pizza and fries,
With every wave, my spirit flies!

Whispers call from the salt-laced breeze,
"Where's your map?" teases the sea tease.
In the vast blue, absurdity rules,
Crazy thoughts float like silly fools!

So here I sail into the unknown,
Adventure calls, I'm never alone!
With laughter loud, I take the leap,
For every voyage, my heart will keep!

Kaleidoscope of Dusk's Embrace

In shadows where the seagulls sing,
A crab wears shades, like it's a king.
The sunset spills like pancake mix,
While jellyfish dance, doing their tricks.

The waves are giggling, oh so sly,
They tickle toes as they rush by.
A sunset's palette, wild and free,
An otter's snicker adds to the spree.

With sandy hats and flip-flop flair,
The palm trees sway without a care.
Each breeze is laughter, soft and light,
As day bids farewell to the night.

The shifting colors tease the eye,
While crabs in moonlight start to fly.
In dusk's embrace, joy takes its place,
We chuckle on in this wild space.

Glimmering Treasures on Twilight's Shore

A starfish wearing sparkly shoes,
Says 'Hello, friend!' with cheerful views.
Old shells gossip, secrets unfurled,
While dolphins' jokes leave waves twirled.

Cast nets for laughter, catch them all,
Bright twinkling treasures on a ball.
The tide brings giggles with each splash,
While seagulls compete in a feathery dash.

A rubber duck floats, bold and free,
Yelling 'Look at me!' with glee.
As shimmery shells hold tales to tell,
The twilight's magic cast a spell.

Each sunset carries a punchy pun,
As conch shells whisper, 'Join the fun!'
On this shore where tides align,
Glimmers of joy are simply divine.

Breezy Escapes in Celestial Symphony

With kites that dance like awkward fish,
The wind hums tunes, granting a wish.
Clouds pirouette in the cobalt sky,
As if they're planning to flutter by.

A picnic planned with sandwiches stacked,
But a seagull swoops and launches an act.
It steals a chip, a cheeky little thief,
Leaving behind tickles of disbelief.

The breeze brings stories from afar,
Of starry journeys and a luckless star.
With laughter rumbling through the trees,
And whispers shared among the leaves.

An orchestra plays with every wave,
A rhythm that invites the brave.
So let us twirl with joy, believe,
In breezy dreams that we can weave.

Lighthouses Guiding Phantom Ships

Tall lighthouses wink with eerie grins,
As phantom ships share tales of sins.
The foghorn's laugh adds to the thrill,
While seaweed twirls in a ghostly chill.

Old mariners tell tales of delight,
Of ghostly lanterns on moonlit nights.
Salty seagulls whisper, set the mood,
As fishermen argue who caught the food.

The tides carry whispers of sailors' cheer,
While mermaids splash to draw us near.
With each glimmer, a secret unfurls,
In midnight frolics, laughter twirls.

Now raise a toast to ships of the past,
As the lighthouse shines, a guardian cast.
In this otherworldly, magical nook,
Where phantoms dance and dreams unhook.

Whims of the Enchanted Ocean

Waves are giggling, making a scene,
Seashells dance, like it's Halloween.
Fish wear sunglasses, oh what a sight,
Seagulls taking selfies, left and right.

Lobsters debating, who's left on the grill,
Crabs moonwalking, showing their skill.
A starfish sings karaoke on sand,
While dolphins play jazz, isn't it grand?

Jellyfish float by with a funky style,
Sharks start a dance-off, go the extra mile.
Turtles slow motion, groovin' just right,
While octopuses juggle all through the night.

Constellations Above the Shimmering Sea

Stars are giggling, way up high,
Making wishes as they pass by.
The moon's wearing shades, a cheeky lad,
While comets crash parties, isn't that rad?

Mermaids are stargazing, sipping on tea,
Bubbling with laughter, carefree as can be.
An octopus plans a festival soon,
With celestial music to hum under the moon.

Sea turtles float with a laugh in their eyes,
While sea urchins tell cheesy surprise.
Who knew the night sky could be such a show?
In a world where laughter and starlight glow!

Unclouded Visions of Endless Blue

The sky is a canvas, splashed with fun,
Clouds are cotton candy, oh what a run!
Seashells gossip about fish in disguise,
While crabs in tuxedos check on their ties.

Pelicans prancing, all dressed up for lunch,
While anemones giggle, quite a bunch.
The sea sparkles, like glitter in sun,
As sea creatures gather for their daily fun.

Tide pools are playgrounds for the sea stars,
With sea cucumbers counting their cars.
The breeze whispers jokes, with a playful tease,
Turning calm waters to a whirl of ease.

Enveloping Calm of Coastal Nights

Nights wrap around like a cozy blanket,
While crickets perform a concert so quaint.
Starfish tell tales to the shells on the shore,
While the moon winks at waves, wanting more.

Coconuts roll by, what a cheeky bunch,
Inviting the sea breeze to join in for lunch.
Laughter echoes off the cliffside so bright,
As lanterns dance gently, a twinkling sight.

The sea murmurs secrets, both funny and wise,
Under a tapestry of shimmering skies.
As night drapes its shawl over laughter and glee,
It's just another wild night by the sea!

Gentle Currents Call

Waves roll in with a playful grin,
As seagulls squawk, they're ready to win.
A crab scuttles by, wearing a hat,
We chuckle and cheer as we all chat.

Shells twinkle like gems on the sandy floor,
One tries to run, but it's really quite sore.
With laughter and joy, the sun starts to dance,
To the rhythm of tides, we all take a chance.

Beneath the Palm's Embrace

Palms sway lightly, a joke in the breeze,
While folks madly scramble, just trying to freeze.
A drink spills over, what a clumsy sight,
Now everyone's giggling, feeling delight.

Sandy toes wiggle in the hot summer air,
As someone yells loudly, "Beware of the chair!"
A sandcastle towers, but it's under attack,
By a dog with a mission: 'That's my snack!'

Lullaby of the Tides

The waves are singing a lullaby sweet,
As beach balls bounce and land at our feet.
A toddler is chasing a wave with great glee,
Only to tumble, oh dear, oh me!

Under the sun, laughter echoes around,
As someone steps boldly, then falls to the ground.
Bikini tops fly as the breeze takes a turn,
With each playful moment, more laughter we earn.

Solace in the Sunlight

Sun's shining bright, but we're all a bit dim,
As our sunscreen battles, we laugh at the whim.
A friend in a hat says, "I'm ready to bake!"
But she's just too crispy; a big joke to make!

Towels laid out, like colorful stripes,
We lounge and we giggle, sharing our gripes.
"Oh please, hold my drink while I take a leap!"
Into the water, splashing everyone deep!

Dreams on the Salted Air

Seagulls squawking, doing a dance,
Chasing after chips, it's a beach romance.
Sandy toes giggle, laughter in the sun,
Ice cream drips down, oh what fun!

Flip-flops flapping, racing for the waves,
Building castles, no time for knaves.
Sand in our sandwiches, what a delight,
Sun-kissed silliness, pure day and night.

Coconuts hiding, a treasure of rum,
Laughter erupts, here comes the fun!
Seashells are singing, making their sound,
In this salty paradise, joy can be found.

Sunset glow paints, a canvas so fine,
We toast to the chaos with fizzy wine.
Dreams on the salted air, oh what a spree,
Life's a simple riddle, just you and me.

Driftwood Tales Beneath the Stars

Driftwood gathered, stories to tell,
Tales of the sea, where troubles fell.
Stars overhead twinkle, a cosmic show,
Fishermen's yarns, from long ago.

Tangled seaweed, hats on our heads,
Crabs join the party, while gossip spreads.
Firelight flickers, like startled fireflies,
Our laughter carries, a night full of sighs.

Splashing water, a splashy retreat,
Bumping into dolphins, quite the treat.
With s'mores in hand and spirits high,
Even the moon can't help but pry.

Under the cosmos, with drinks and snacks,
The night wears on, and humor lacks.
Driftwood tales told beneath the stars,
In moments of mirth, we forget our scars.

A Journey with Sailor's Breath

With a captain's hat and a wink of glee,
We sail the waters, wild and free.
The wind's a joker, playing tricks all day,
Knocking off schedules, but we're okay!

Fish in the cooler say 'How do you do?'
While seagulls debate who's got the best view.
With compass spinning, we're lost, oh well,
Singing loud shanties, to cast a spell.

The anchor dances, it's a wobbly mess,
We laugh like pirates, in our own jest.
A journey with spirit, a merry-go-round,
Adventure's our mantra, wherever we're bound.

As the sun dips low, we toast to the day,
With soggy baguettes, we laugh all the way.
Sailor's breath whispers, "Let's do it again!"
In the comedy of waves, we're always the best friends.

Fragments of Light on Wistful Waters

Moonlit ripples, a wobbly boat,
The frogs have gathered, singing their note.
Fireflies buzz like they own the night,
Splashing in puddles, what a funny sight!

Plenty of snacks, but who took the cake?
The raccoons gather for a late-night break.
Each splash and stumble, a giggle erupts,
Fragments of laughter, the night corrupts.

Stars throw confetti, in a twinkling fight,
Paddles are clumsy, oh, what a fright!
The owls are hooting, "What's all the fuss?"
But joy is contagious, like a glittery gust.

Fragments of light on wistful streams,
We sail with hilarity, living our dreams.
With cheeky critters and shimmered delight,
Tonight, we're bound by humor's flight.

Sojourn of the Wayward Wind

A gust came by with quite a grin,
It tickled palms and teased my chin.
I chased it down, to my surprise,
It led me straight to coconut pies.

The seagulls laughed, they stole my hat,
I yelled, they screeched, 'You're such a brat!'
But as they danced on salty air,
I joined their waltz—no time to care.

A flip-flop flew, took off like a kite,
I ran and stumbled, what a sight!
The wind just giggled, spun me around,
While I tripped over seashells on the ground.

At sunset's glow, I found my fate,
Stuck in sand, oh, isn't that great?
With laughter echoing through the night,
I toasted to my wobbly flight.

Fluid Journeys on Gentle Currents

Rafts of leaf drift on the bay,
While turtles laugh, they shout, 'Hooray!'
With snacks on board, the feast begins,
As crabs applaud my awkward spins.

The water's warm, it hugs my toes,
And flippered fish strike silly poses.
I reach for chips, they swat my hand,
A finned revolt, oh, isn't it grand?

My floaty squeaks, a merry tune,
As gulls dive bomb like cartoon goons.
With every splash and playful sway,
I find my joy in this raucous play.

As sun dips down and day takes flight,
I call for snacks—what a delight!
I float into the twilight's gleam,
Content and silly, lost in a dream.

Adrift in the Caressing Calm

I drift alone on a rubber raft,
Where jellyfish spin like an art craft.
They wave their tentacles, 'Join our game!'
I'm laughing hard, it's never the same.

A crab in shades tips his hat,
He's quite the fella, imagine that!
Together we sip on juices bright,
While mermaids wink under moonlight.

A floating parade of oddball fish,
Served up my salad—oh, what a dish!
They jived and grooved to a sea shanty,
Even the starfish joined in, fancy!

As I drift on, the laughter swells,
With sandy tales, and ocean spells.
What a ride on this whimsy spree,
Forever in stitches, oh, can't you see?

Bibliophile of the Beachfront Muse

With a book in hand, I lounge in sand,
As sea breezes toss my pages—and!
Giggling kids run by with glee,
'A bookworm's snack? A crab's decree!'

Sandcastles rise amid my tale,
While seagulls plot a crafty sail.
Little did I know, they want to read,
The joy they find in every bead.

Each chapter winds with laughter loud,
As ocean waves come, proud and proud.
The plots twist up and down that shore,
I close the book, and then I soar.

Under the sun, I laugh and sip,
My thoughts adrift on a joyful trip.
With salty winds and a plot so fine,
What a beach day, all mine, all mine!

Between Sunsets and Secrets

The sun dips low, the beach is hot,
A treasure hunt? I think I forgot.
With flip-flops flying, I chase my hat,
While seagulls squawk like they're holding a spat.

With palm trees swaying, it's hard to think,
I spilled my drink and it started to sink.
A crab steals my sandwich, I chase it around,
In this wacky world, who's the fool to be found?

Sunburns are red, like my laughter tonight,
As friends tell their stories, each one takes flight.
The tide rolls in, with it, our cheer,
Let's dance 'til dawn, with nary a fear!

So raise your glasses, let's make a toast,
To the tales we weave, and the friendship we boast.
Under colorful skies, we'll share our delight,
Between sunsets and secrets, let's party all night!

Lucid Chants of Ocean Spray

The waves are singing a quirky tune,
While jellyfish dance beneath the moon.
I put on sunscreen, as a seagull shrieks,
Its laughter echoes, well, let's just say it speaks.

A surfboard's my ride, but I'm stuck on dry,
With my balance gone, I look like a fly.
The ocean calls, but I'm stuck in a whirl,
My adventures turn wacky when 'surf's up' unfurl.

Flip-flops are flinging as I haphazardly run,
Chasing after crabs who seem to have fun.
A splash here, a splash there, I'm soaked to the bone,
This seaside circus sure feels like home.

But laughter just bubbles, and joy fills the air,
For every mishap, there's fun to share.
With salty kisses from waves we embrace,
In lucid chants of this splashy race!

Sails Swaying Amidst Island Dreams

Sails are swaying, catching the breeze,
But I'm stuck in knots, brought to my knees!
A parrot on my shoulder squawks, 'What a mess!'
I wink back and say, 'You're no more than a pest!'

The horizon shimmers, our map's gone awry,
I aim for a snack but hit a seagull pie.
With laughter erupting from the crew on deck,
The ocean rolls up and gives us a check!

Crooked compasses and stories they weave,
As jellyfish giggle and sea turtles grieve.
Though sailboats are meant to float in the bliss,
It's hard not to chuckle at the chaos like this!

So I raise my drink to the hiccups we face,
Underneath a grand sky, we're lost in our place.
With sails swaying 'round, we float through the gleams,
Living our days in these whimsical dreams!

Erasing Footprints in Sugar Sands

The sugar sands glisten, but oh, what a mess,
My bucket spills syrup, can't clean up the dress!
With laughter and giggles, my toes are a riot,
As the tide rolls in, it's a comical riot.

Chasing the waves, I trip on my feet,
In and out of the water, a bittersweet feat.
Collecting some shells, but they're all quite shy,
Hiding behind rocks, as I pass them by.

Crabs in their armor scuttle with glee,
I try to be stealthy, yet trip on a bee.
With every step forward, the sand says, 'Not yet!',
Erasing my footprints, my laugh I can't vet!

So let's raise a cheer for the sweet sandy fights,
Foamy waves crashing, oh what funny sights!
In the tangy sea air, let friendship expand,
As we erase footprints in sugar-soft sand!

Rustic Beauty of the Sea Escape

The sand is warm, the sun's a tease,
I lost my hat, caught by a breeze.
Seagulls squawk as I take a dip,
They laugh at me; I'm taking a trip.

A crab's got my sandwich, oh how rude,
He's dancing away, in a crabby mood.
The waves roll in, they splash and play,
While I trip over them, though I sway.

Shells washed up like treasures from lore,
Each one a story I can't ignore.
With laughter echoing in the air,
Sun-kissed skin, no troubles to bear.

So here I am, living my best,
Chasing jellyfish, a curious quest.
Here's to the sea, where fun's in the mix,
Rustic beauty, my home away fix.

Land's End Lullabies

At land's end, the seagulls sing,
I mime the notes; it's awkward bling.
The salt in the air, it tickles my nose,
I sneeze so loud, the beach party slows.

Beach balls bouncing, I try to catch,
They fly over me, oh what a match!
With kids running, all laughter and squeals,
I'm dodging beach hats, that's how it feels.

The tide keeps coming, with a wink and a nod,
I slip in the foam, give the water a prod.
With a splash and a giggle, I can't help but play,
But watch out! Here comes my sandwich buffet.

As sunbeams tickle, I sway with the breeze,
Life's simple pleasures bring me to my knees.
Land's end is funny, with tales fresh and bright,
In this lullaby, I'll dance through the night.

Tides of Tranquility

The tides roll in, whisper soft and low,
I build castles, but they just won't grow.
A pail full of hopes, just spills on the ground,
As waves come crashing, my dreams aren't found.

My flip-flops are missing, where can they be?
Oh wait, they're swimming! How can that be?
With each goofy step, I trip and I slide,
Sure, it's hilarious! Just don't let it ride.

The seashells giggle as I pick them all up,
But one bites my finger; oh what a pup!
I toss it aside, it flies like a rocket,
Fools the tide, and runs off with my pocket.

Yet through all the chaos, my heart's full of glee,
This dance with the waves, it's just so carefree.
In tides of tranquility, laughter's the key,
With splashes of fun, I'm as wild as can be.

Horizon's Embrace

The horizon waves, with a wink of the sun,
I take a big leap, but oh, I can't run!
With noodles for legs, I flop like a fish,
Everyone's laughing, it's just my big wish.

Leaping towards waves with a splash and a cheer,
The water's so chilly; I scream, "Oh dear!"
A dolphin swims by, gives a cheeky grin,
As I flounder about—oh, where have I been?

With surfboards galore, they slide on the swell,
I try my hand; I'm a story to tell.
A twist and a twirl, I fall on my back,
The ocean laughs loud; I'm under attack!

The sunset arrives, with colors profound,
I wave to the sky, and king crabs abound.
In horizon's embrace, joy takes the stage,
With fun so contagious, I'll turn up the page.

Serenities Wrapped in Salty Embrace

Oh, how the gulls squawk high in glee,
While sandy toes dance at the edge of the sea.
A jellyfish floats, quite lost in thought,
I ponder my snack, but it's way too hot.

The sunscreen's a battle, it's sticky and thick,
As seagulls dive down, oh what a trick!
My drink's just a sipper, now half on my lap,
Is this a vacation or just a mishap?

Flip-flops are flopping, they reek of the tide,
But who needs style? I'm here for the ride!
With laughter and sandcastles as tall as a tree,
I'm the king of the beach — just don't look at me!

Yet as day turns to dusk, the colors ignite,
I chuckle at waves on the edge of the night.
With humor in tides and the stars shining bright,
I'll dance with the dolphins — but only in spite!

A Dance with the Wandering Wave

Oh, my surfboard's a noodle, it slips and it slides,
I waddle and giggle, no one can abide.
With each little tumble, I'm rising to greet,
The water's a bouncer — come join my defeat!

The waves take my worries, they wash them away,
But my flip-flop just launched — oh, what a ballet!
I paddle out bravely, what could go wrong?
But a crab snaps my toe, and I'm gone in a throng!

The surf is a circus, and I'm the main act,
With each splash and chortle, there's laughter intact.
Every wave is a giggle, every splash is a cheer,
Call me the jester, I have nothing to fear!

Yet daydreams abound as the sun starts to set,
I try for the big one, but fall with a let.
With foam in my hair and sand on my face,
I stand up to bow — it's a clam-funny race!

Secrets in the Still of Evening

As twilight unveils with a wink and a grin,
The ocean spills secrets, where do I begin?
A crab moonwalks sideways, what's under its shell?
I tiptoe in laughter — oh, do tell, do tell!

The coconut drinks are a bit on the strong,
As I slosh in the sand singing off-key, what a song!
The stars twinkle back, with a gleaming delight,
Whispering jokes only the night can incite.

With laughter so bright, like the fireflies' dance,
I trip over shadows in this silly romance.
The night is eternal, yet time ticks away,
I'll be here forever, or at least 'til the day!

The waves whisper softly, 'Come join us for fun,'
With grins and with giggles, the evening's begun.
So let's make a toast — to the crazy and free,
Here's to goofy nights on the edge of the sea!

Horizons Unfurling Skyward

With colors exploding in a carnival hue,
I look to the horizon — oh, what a view!
But up in the sky, a bird steals my snack,
I chase it in jest, but it flies — oh, it's whack!

The sun plays a game, peeking in and out,
While sand dollars giggle, there's dancing about.
The fish on the line seem to tease and to taunt,
But I'm busy being the beachwear savant!

With laughter and giggles, we build tall and proud,
Sandcastles that sparkle — hey, aren't we loud?
I spill my soda; it fizzles away,
While friends roll in laughter, what a display!

Now shadows grow long as the sun sinks so low,
We dance in the twilight, oh, go with the flow!
With joyous companions, let time whisk away,
As horizons unfold in a bright, silly play!

Whispers from the Distant Coves

Seagulls gossip high above,
Sneaky crabs dance with a shove.
Turtles wear their shades in style,
While the fish swim with a smile.

The sunfish throw a beach party,
While conchs sing tunes that are hearty.
Jellyfish groove, floating with flair,
And the starfish model without a care.

Loud laughter echoes from the shore,
As the clams argue over who's more.
Kites tangled up in coconut trees,
Oh, the slapstick of ocean's breeze!

With flip-flops flying, the kids retreat,
A sandcastle's lost to the playful heat.
The tide comes in with a splashing roar,
And the clumsy surfboard hits the floor!

Chasing Shadows on Sandy Pathways

Beach balls thump through the air,
While laughter mixes with sun's glare.
Children chasing each wave's tease,
Their sandy toes stuck like cheese!

Sunbathers flipping like pancakes,
While surfboards practice their fakes.
The sunburned crab yells, "Hey, you!"
As the lifeguard snoozes, oh boo-hoo!

Flip-flops squeak, a natural sound,
As they race 'round on the ground.
Seashells play hide-and-seek with sand,
While seagulls plot a food heist so grand!

But wait! What's that? A splashing fuss,
It's just a dog causing a fuss.
Oh, watch your cheese dip, don't let it drown!
On this wacky beach, where fun is renowned!

Swaying Palms and Ocean's Call

Palms sway like dancers in glee,
While the breeze teases, 'Come dance with me!'
Coconuts fall with a comical thump,
As watermelon rolls with a plump.

The waves whisper tales of the deep,
While beach umbrellas stand in a heap.
Sandy toes dip for a quick splash,
As the sunburned tourist takes a crash!

With fresh coconut drinks piled high,
Parrots squawk tales that make you cry.
Sandcastles lean after the wave's kiss,
And everyone giggles, "What did we miss?"

A crab steals a sandwich, a daring feat,
While beachgoers laugh at their own defeat.
Under the sun, where the fun's never small,
Life tickles you, just like a beach ball!

Awakening in the Coastal Glow

Roosters crow while the sunrise winks,
As the coffee pot, brightly clinks.
Waves gently whisper good morning cheer,
While dolphins laugh, 'We're swimming here!'

Bikers zoom with a sea-salt grin,
While surfers wait for the dawn to begin.
The fisherman's line gets caught in a vine,
As seagulls squawk, "That's not as fine!"

Little kids with their giggles loud,
Building forts, feeling oh so proud.
A sunhat flies as the wind talks back,
Creating moments of comedic knack!

As the sun rises, the fun just starts,
With flip-flops and laughter, we play our parts.
In this coastal land where worries are few,
Awake to the joy, the playful renew!

Flickers of Daydreams on Coral Shores

Seagulls gossip with careless squawks,
Under the sun where the flip-flop walks.
Crabs do the cha-cha on sandy stage,
While sandcastles fall, like forgotten page.

Tropical drinks spill with a splashy cheer,
As sunburned tourists shout 'I hold my beer!'
Jellyfish dance like they own the place,
And sunhats get snatched in a clumsy chase.

Ice cream melts, as the sun takes a beat,
Kids build a fortress, then claim defeat.
With every wave, laughter rises high,
Though umbrellas fly like kites in the sky.

And when the night comes, stars in the sea,
We'll toast to the fact that we're all quite free.
For here on these shores, where the antics increase,
Life's a big joke, and we're laughing in peace.

Horizons Steeped in Solitude

On a hammock strung between two palm trees,
A squirrel yells, 'Hey, could you not sneeze?'
Birds serenade with hilarious tones,
While lazy cats steal our sunburned bones.

A crab throws shade with a sassy wave,
Counting the waves like it's how to behave.
Seaglass shines, and my thoughts drift far,
Should we chase the moon, or just drink from a jar?

What's that on the horizon? Not sure, my friend,
Just a litter of flip-flops, the day's perfect blend.
Lost in the nonsense of dubious dreams,
Where nothing is urgent, or so it seems.

And rushing around feels like a circus act,
Under the skies where no plans are unpacked.
So here's to this snooze, this whimsical plight,
Tomorrow's for chores; tonight, we'll take flight.

Swirls of Laughter and Lapping Tides

Waves clap together like friends in a brawl,
While beach balls bounce as they answer the call.
Frogs in tuxedos croak at the moon,
As the fish flash smiles—it's a peculiar tune.

Surfboards flip, and the beach towels fly,
While sunscreen wars break out under the sky.
A tourist drops chips, and the seagulls dive,
At the feast of the foolish, the foolish survive.

Sunburnt noses play peek-a-boo games,
Shelling out laughter while nobody aims.
As jellyfish giggle with their soft, squishy glee,
We frolic like dolphins, so wild and so free.

Every splash brings a burst of delight,
In this wacky realm where weird feels just right.
So gather your giggles, let's ride this grand tide,
'Cause the laughter we share is the best kind of glide.

The Allure of Soft Tropical Winds

A breeze tickles noses, a playful tease,
As flip-flops gather, like old chums at ease.
Parrots converse in colorful slang,
While sunburned limbs let out a loud clang.

Around every corner, a joke's in the air,
With sand in our toes and sun-kissed hair.
Picnic blankets filled with mishaps galore,
A sandwich escapes, who could ask for more?

As waves offer whispers, and seashells sing,
Even crabs throw shade to see what we bring.
Bamboo umbrellas sway in a laugh,
While fruit cocktails wobble, a bubbly gaffe.

When night rolls in, the fireflies tease,
Flipping our worries to the whims of the breeze.
With giggles and snacks, let's toast to our plight,
For life is a laugh on these shores bright with light.

www.ingramcontent.com/pod-product-compliance
Lightning Source LLC
Chambersburg PA
CBHW072131070526
44585CB00016B/1628